45 Keto-Friendly Recipes for Home

By: Kelly Johnson

Table of Contents

- Keto Avocado and Bacon Egg Cups
- Cauliflower Crust Pizza
- Zucchini Noodles with Pesto and Cherry Tomatoes
- Keto Chicken Alfredo with Broccoli
- Eggplant Lasagna
- Keto Butter Burgers
- Salmon with Lemon Dill Butter Sauce
- Keto Chicken Caesar Salad
- Cabbage Rolls with Ground Beef and Cauliflower Rice
- Keto Shrimp Scampi
- Bacon-wrapped Asparagus Bundles
- Keto Meatball Subs with Almond Flour Bread
- Creamy Garlic Parmesan Brussels Sprouts
- Keto Beef and Broccoli Stir-Fry
- Spinach and Feta Stuffed Chicken Breast
- Keto Taco Salad with Ground Turkey
- Sausage and Egg Breakfast Casserole
- Keto Broccoli Cheddar Soup
- Avocado and Bacon Stuffed Mushrooms
- Keto Cauliflower Mac and Cheese
- Grilled Lemon Herb Chicken Thighs
- Keto Egg Drop Soup
- Cauliflower Fried Rice
- Keto Tuna Salad Lettuce Wraps
- Cheesy Bacon-Wrapped Jalapeño Poppers
- Keto Buffalo Chicken Dip
- Spaghetti Squash with Pesto and Cherry Tomatoes
- Keto Chicken Zoodle Soup
- Baked Parmesan Crusted Salmon
- Keto Avocado Chocolate Pudding
- Low-Carb Zucchini Bread
- Keto Cauliflower Hummus
- Creamy Garlic Parmesan Shrimp
- Keto Chocolate Avocado Smoothie
- Cabbage and Sausage Skillet

- Keto Broccoli and Cheese Stuffed Chicken Breast
- Avocado Bacon and Egg Salad
- Zucchini Noodles with Creamy Alfredo Sauce
- Keto Lemon Blueberry Cheesecake Bars
- Cauliflower Tots
- Keto Garlic Butter Shrimp
- Keto Chicken Fajita Bowls
- Cheesy Cauliflower Breadsticks
- Keto Chocolate Peanut Butter Fat Bombs
- Grilled Portobello Mushrooms with Balsamic Glaze

Keto Avocado and Bacon Egg Cups

Ingredients:

- 2 ripe avocados, halved and pitted
- 4 large eggs
- 4 slices of bacon, cooked until crispy
- Salt and pepper, to taste
- Fresh chives or parsley, chopped (for garnish, optional)

Instructions:

Preheat the Oven:
- Preheat your oven to 375°F (190°C).

Prepare Avocado Halves:
- Use a spoon to scoop out a small portion of the flesh from each avocado half, creating a larger well for the egg. Place the avocados in a baking dish to keep them stable.

Crack Eggs into Avocados:
- Carefully crack one egg into each avocado half, ensuring the yolk fits within the well you created. Season each egg with a pinch of salt and pepper.

Bake:
- Place the baking dish in the preheated oven and bake for about 12-15 minutes or until the egg whites are set, but the yolks are still slightly runny. Adjust the baking time based on your desired egg doneness.

Cook Bacon:
- While the eggs are baking, cook the bacon until crispy. Once cooked, chop or crumble the bacon into small pieces.

Top with Bacon:
- Once the eggs are done, remove the baking dish from the oven. Sprinkle the cooked bacon pieces over the eggs.

Garnish and Serve:
- Garnish with chopped fresh chives or parsley, if desired. Serve the Keto Avocado and Bacon Egg Cups immediately.

Enjoy:
- Scoop out the creamy avocado and egg mixture with a spoon, making sure to get a bit of bacon in each bite.

These Keto Avocado and Bacon Egg Cups make for a delicious and satisfying breakfast or brunch. The combination of creamy avocado, perfectly baked eggs, and crispy bacon creates a flavorful and filling dish that aligns with a keto-friendly lifestyle.

Cauliflower Crust Pizza

Ingredients:

For the Cauliflower Crust:

- 1 medium-sized cauliflower head, riced (about 4 cups)
- 1 large egg
- 1 cup shredded mozzarella cheese
- 1/4 cup grated Parmesan cheese
- 1 teaspoon dried oregano
- 1/2 teaspoon garlic powder
- Salt and pepper, to taste

For Toppings:

- 1/2 cup sugar-free pizza sauce
- 1 1/2 cups shredded mozzarella cheese
- Your favorite pizza toppings (e.g., pepperoni, olives, mushrooms, bell peppers)

Instructions:

For the Cauliflower Crust:

Preheat the Oven:
- Preheat your oven to 425°F (220°C). Place a pizza stone or a baking sheet in the oven while it preheats.

Prepare the Cauliflower:
- Wash and dry the cauliflower head. Cut it into florets, and then use a food processor to rice the cauliflower until it resembles fine crumbs.

Cook the Cauliflower:
- Place the riced cauliflower in a microwave-safe bowl and microwave on high for 4-5 minutes, or until it's cooked. Allow it to cool for a few minutes.

Squeeze Out Moisture:
- Transfer the cooked cauliflower to a clean kitchen towel or cheesecloth. Squeeze out as much moisture as possible. This step is crucial for a crispy crust.

Mix the Crust Ingredients:
- In a bowl, combine the squeezed cauliflower, egg, shredded mozzarella, Parmesan, oregano, garlic powder, salt, and pepper. Mix until well combined.

Form the Crust:
- Place a piece of parchment paper on a flat surface. Spread the cauliflower mixture onto the parchment paper, forming a round pizza crust.

Bake the Crust:
- Carefully transfer the parchment paper with the crust onto the preheated pizza stone or baking sheet. Bake for 12-15 minutes or until the crust is golden brown and firm.

Add Toppings:
- Remove the crust from the oven and spread sugar-free pizza sauce over the surface. Sprinkle shredded mozzarella cheese and your favorite toppings.

Bake Again:
- Return the pizza to the oven and bake for an additional 10-12 minutes or until the cheese is melted and bubbly.

Slice and Serve:
- Allow the cauliflower crust pizza to cool slightly before slicing. Serve and enjoy your low-carb pizza!

This Cauliflower Crust Pizza is a tasty and keto-friendly alternative that allows you to enjoy pizza without the traditional carb-heavy crust. Feel free to get creative with your toppings for a personalized and satisfying pizza experience.

Zucchini Noodles with Pesto and Cherry Tomatoes

Ingredients:

For Zucchini Noodles:

- 4 medium-sized zucchinis, spiralized into noodles
- 1 tablespoon olive oil
- Salt and pepper, to taste

For Pesto:

- 2 cups fresh basil leaves, packed
- 1/2 cup grated Parmesan cheese
- 1/2 cup pine nuts or walnuts, toasted
- 2 garlic cloves
- 1/2 cup extra-virgin olive oil
- Salt and pepper, to taste

For Assembly:

- 1 cup cherry tomatoes, halved
- Extra Parmesan cheese, for garnish (optional)

Instructions:

For Zucchini Noodles:

Prepare Zucchini Noodles:
- Spiralize the zucchinis into noodles using a spiralizer. If you don't have a spiralizer, you can use a vegetable peeler to create ribbon-like noodles.

Cook Zucchini Noodles:
- Heat olive oil in a large pan over medium heat. Add the zucchini noodles and sauté for 2-3 minutes until they are just tender but still have a slight crunch. Season with salt and pepper.

Drain Excess Moisture:
- If the zucchini noodles release excess moisture, you can drain it by placing them in a colander and pressing down gently with a paper towel.

For Pesto:

Make Pesto:

- In a food processor, combine basil, grated Parmesan, toasted pine nuts or walnuts, and garlic cloves. Pulse until the ingredients are finely chopped.

Add Olive Oil:
- With the food processor running, slowly pour in the extra-virgin olive oil until the pesto reaches your desired consistency. Season with salt and pepper to taste.

For Assembly:

Toss Zoodles with Pesto:
- In the pan with the cooked zucchini noodles, add the freshly prepared pesto. Toss the noodles until they are evenly coated with the pesto.

Add Cherry Tomatoes:
- Gently fold in the halved cherry tomatoes.

Serve:
- Transfer the Zucchini Noodles with Pesto and Cherry Tomatoes to serving plates. Optionally, garnish with extra Parmesan cheese.

Enjoy:
- Serve immediately and enjoy this light and flavorful low-carb dish!

This Zucchini Noodles with Pesto and Cherry Tomatoes recipe is not only delicious but also packed with nutrients. It's a perfect option for those looking for a lighter and carb-conscious alternative to traditional pasta dishes.

Keto Chicken Alfredo with Broccoli

Ingredients:

For the Chicken and Broccoli:

- 2 boneless, skinless chicken breasts, thinly sliced
- Salt and pepper, to taste
- 2 tablespoons olive oil
- 2 cups broccoli florets

For the Alfredo Sauce:

- 1/2 cup unsalted butter
- 1 cup heavy cream
- 1 cup grated Parmesan cheese
- 2 cloves garlic, minced
- Salt and pepper, to taste
- 1/2 teaspoon nutmeg (optional)

For Serving:

- Zucchini noodles or other keto-friendly noodles (optional)
- Fresh parsley, chopped (for garnish)

Instructions:

For the Chicken and Broccoli:

 Cook Chicken:
- Season thinly sliced chicken breasts with salt and pepper. In a large skillet, heat olive oil over medium-high heat. Add the chicken slices and cook until browned on both sides and fully cooked. Remove the chicken from the skillet and set aside.

 Steam Broccoli:
- In the same skillet, add broccoli florets. You can add a splash of water and cover the skillet to steam the broccoli until it's tender-crisp. Remove the broccoli and set aside.

For the Alfredo Sauce:

 Prepare Alfredo Sauce:

- In the skillet, melt the butter over medium heat. Add minced garlic and sauté until fragrant.

Add Heavy Cream:
- Pour in the heavy cream and bring it to a simmer. Reduce the heat to low.

Stir in Parmesan Cheese:
- Gradually whisk in the grated Parmesan cheese, stirring continuously until the sauce is smooth and creamy.

Season:
- Season the Alfredo sauce with salt, pepper, and nutmeg (if using). Adjust the seasoning to your taste.

For Serving:

Combine Chicken, Broccoli, and Sauce:
- Add the cooked chicken and steamed broccoli back into the skillet with the Alfredo sauce. Toss everything together until the chicken and broccoli are evenly coated with the sauce.

Serve Over Keto-Friendly Noodles (Optional):
- If desired, serve the Keto Chicken Alfredo over zucchini noodles or your favorite keto-friendly noodles.

Garnish and Enjoy:
- Garnish with fresh chopped parsley and additional Parmesan cheese. Serve immediately.

This Keto Chicken Alfredo with Broccoli is a creamy and flavorful dish that's rich in fats and low in carbs, making it a perfect option for a keto-friendly meal. Adjust the ingredients and portion sizes based on your dietary preferences and needs.

Eggplant Lasagna

Ingredients:

For the Eggplant Layers:

- 2 medium-sized eggplants, thinly sliced lengthwise
- Salt, for sweating the eggplant

For the Meat Sauce:

- 1 pound ground beef or Italian sausage
- 1 onion, finely chopped
- 2 cloves garlic, minced
- 1 can (14 oz) crushed tomatoes
- 1 can (6 oz) tomato paste
- 1 teaspoon dried oregano
- 1 teaspoon dried basil
- Salt and pepper, to taste

For the Cheese Filling:

- 1 cup ricotta cheese
- 1 cup shredded mozzarella cheese
- 1/2 cup grated Parmesan cheese
- 1 large egg
- 2 tablespoons fresh basil, chopped
- Salt and pepper, to taste

Additional Layers:

- 1 1/2 cups shredded mozzarella cheese
- 1/2 cup grated Parmesan cheese
- Fresh basil or parsley, chopped (for garnish)

Instructions:

For the Eggplant Layers:

    Preheat Oven:
- Preheat your oven to 375°F (190°C).

    Sweat the Eggplant:

- Place the eggplant slices on a baking sheet, sprinkle with salt, and let them sit for about 15-20 minutes. This helps draw out excess moisture.

Pat Dry:
- Pat the eggplant slices dry with paper towels to remove the released moisture.

Roast Eggplant:
- Arrange the eggplant slices on baking sheets and roast in the preheated oven for about 15-20 minutes, or until they are tender. Remove from the oven and set aside.

For the Meat Sauce:

Cook Meat:
- In a large skillet, brown the ground beef or Italian sausage over medium heat. Drain excess fat if needed.

Add Onion and Garlic:
- Add chopped onions and minced garlic to the skillet. Cook until the onions are softened.

Add Tomatoes and Seasoning:
- Stir in crushed tomatoes, tomato paste, dried oregano, dried basil, salt, and pepper. Simmer for about 10-15 minutes to allow the flavors to meld.

For the Cheese Filling:

Prepare Cheese Mixture:
- In a bowl, mix ricotta cheese, shredded mozzarella, grated Parmesan, egg, chopped fresh basil, salt, and pepper.

Assembling the Lasagna:

Layer the Lasagna:
- In a greased baking dish, start by spreading a layer of meat sauce. Place a layer of roasted eggplant slices on top. Add a layer of the cheese mixture. Repeat the layers until all ingredients are used, finishing with a layer of meat sauce on top.

Top with Cheese:
- Sprinkle shredded mozzarella and grated Parmesan over the top layer.

Bake:
- Bake in the preheated oven for 25-30 minutes or until the cheese is melted and bubbly, and the lasagna is heated through.

Garnish and Serve:
- Garnish with chopped fresh basil or parsley. Allow the lasagna to rest for a few minutes before slicing.

Enjoy:

- Serve and enjoy your Keto Eggplant Lasagna!

This Eggplant Lasagna is a flavorful and satisfying low-carb alternative to traditional lasagna. The roasted eggplant adds a delicious layer of texture, and the cheesy filling and meat sauce bring all the flavors together.

Keto Butter Burgers

Ingredients:

For the Burger Patties:

- 1.5 pounds ground beef (preferably 80% lean)
- Salt and pepper, to taste
- 4 slices of cheddar or your favorite keto-friendly cheese (optional)

For the Butter Topping:

- 4 tablespoons unsalted butter, softened
- 2 cloves garlic, minced
- 1 tablespoon fresh parsley, chopped
- Salt and pepper, to taste

For Serving:

- Lettuce leaves or keto-friendly burger buns
- Additional toppings like sliced tomatoes, pickles, and lettuce (optional)

Instructions:

For the Burger Patties:

Shape the Patties:
- Divide the ground beef into 4 equal portions and shape them into burger patties. Season both sides with salt and pepper.

Cook the Patties:
- Heat a skillet or grill pan over medium-high heat. Cook the burger patties for about 3-4 minutes per side or until they reach your preferred level of doneness. If using cheese, add a slice to each patty during the last minute of cooking, allowing it to melt.

Rest the Patties:
- Once cooked, remove the patties from the heat and let them rest while you prepare the butter topping.

For the Butter Topping:

Prepare Butter Mixture:
- In a bowl, combine softened butter, minced garlic, chopped parsley, salt, and pepper. Mix well until the ingredients are evenly incorporated.

Top the Burgers:
- Spoon a generous dollop of the garlic butter mixture onto each burger patty, allowing it to melt and coat the patties.

For Serving:

Prepare Burger Base:
- If you're going for a bun-less option, place each burger patty on a lettuce leaf. Alternatively, use keto-friendly burger buns.

Add Toppings:
- Customize your Keto Butter Burgers with additional toppings like sliced tomatoes, pickles, and lettuce.

Serve and Enjoy:
- Serve the burgers immediately while the garlic butter is still melting. Enjoy the rich and flavorful taste of Keto Butter Burgers!

These Keto Butter Burgers are a delicious and satisfying option for those following a low-carb or ketogenic diet. The garlic butter topping adds a luxurious touch, making these burgers a flavorful and indulgent treat.

Salmon with Lemon Dill Butter Sauce

Ingredients:

For the Salmon:

- 4 salmon fillets
- Salt and pepper, to taste
- Olive oil, for cooking

For the Lemon Dill Butter Sauce:

- 1/2 cup unsalted butter
- 3 tablespoons fresh lemon juice
- 2 tablespoons fresh dill, chopped
- 2 cloves garlic, minced
- Salt and pepper, to taste

Instructions:

For the Salmon:

Preheat Oven:
- Preheat your oven to 400°F (200°C).

Season Salmon:
- Pat the salmon fillets dry with paper towels. Season both sides with salt and pepper.

Sear Salmon:
- Heat olive oil in an oven-safe skillet over medium-high heat. Sear the salmon fillets, skin side up, for about 2-3 minutes until golden brown.

Transfer to Oven:
- Flip the salmon fillets so that the skin side is down. Transfer the skillet to the preheated oven and bake for about 10-12 minutes or until the salmon is cooked through and flakes easily with a fork.

For the Lemon Dill Butter Sauce:

Prepare Sauce:
- In a small saucepan, melt the butter over medium heat.

Add Lemon Juice and Garlic:
- Add fresh lemon juice and minced garlic to the melted butter. Stir well.

Add Dill:

- Stir in the chopped fresh dill. Allow the sauce to simmer for 1-2 minutes to infuse the flavors.

Season:
- Season the sauce with salt and pepper to taste. Adjust the seasoning according to your preference.

Assemble and Serve:

Serve Salmon:
- Remove the salmon fillets from the oven and place them on serving plates.

Pour Sauce:
- Drizzle the Lemon Dill Butter Sauce over the salmon fillets.

Garnish:
- Garnish with additional fresh dill for a burst of color and flavor.

Serve and Enjoy:
- Serve the Salmon with Lemon Dill Butter Sauce immediately, accompanied by your favorite side dishes.

This Salmon with Lemon Dill Butter Sauce is a quick and elegant dish that's perfect for a weeknight dinner or a special occasion. The combination of citrusy lemon, aromatic dill, and rich butter complements the natural flavors of the salmon, creating a delicious and well-balanced meal.

Keto Chicken Caesar Salad

Ingredients:

For the Chicken:

- 2 boneless, skinless chicken breasts
- Salt and pepper, to taste
- 1 tablespoon olive oil
- 1 teaspoon dried oregano
- 1 teaspoon garlic powder

For the Caesar Salad:

- Romaine lettuce, washed and chopped
- 1/2 cup grated Parmesan cheese
- Keto-friendly Caesar dressing (store-bought or homemade)
- Keto-friendly croutons (optional)
- Lemon wedges, for garnish (optional)

Instructions:

For the Chicken:

Season Chicken:
- Season the chicken breasts with salt, pepper, dried oregano, and garlic powder on both sides.

Cook Chicken:
- In a skillet over medium-high heat, heat olive oil. Cook the chicken breasts for about 6-8 minutes per side or until cooked through and no longer pink in the center. The cooking time may vary depending on the thickness of the chicken breasts.

Rest and Slice:
- Remove the chicken from the skillet and let it rest for a few minutes. Slice the chicken into thin strips.

For the Caesar Salad:

Prepare Salad Base:
- In a large bowl, combine the chopped romaine lettuce and grated Parmesan cheese.

Add Chicken:
- Arrange the sliced chicken strips on top of the lettuce and Parmesan.

Drizzle with Dressing:
- Drizzle the Keto-friendly Caesar dressing over the salad. Use as much or as little dressing as you prefer.

Optional Croutons:
- If you're using keto-friendly croutons, sprinkle them over the salad for added crunch.

Toss Gently:
- Gently toss the salad to ensure the ingredients are evenly coated with the dressing.

Garnish and Serve:
- Optionally, garnish with additional grated Parmesan cheese and lemon wedges for a fresh burst of citrus flavor.

Serve Immediately:
- Serve the Keto Chicken Caesar Salad immediately, and enjoy your delicious and low-carb meal!

This Keto Chicken Caesar Salad is a great option for a quick and satisfying lunch or dinner. The combination of crisp romaine lettuce, flavorful grilled chicken, and creamy Caesar dressing makes for a delicious and fulfilling keto-friendly dish.

Cabbage Rolls with Ground Beef and Cauliflower Rice

Ingredients:

For the Cabbage Rolls:

- 1 large head of cabbage
- 1 pound ground beef
- 1/2 cup cauliflower rice (finely chopped cauliflower)
- 1/2 onion, finely chopped
- 2 cloves garlic, minced
- 1 egg
- 1 teaspoon dried oregano
- Salt and pepper, to taste

For the Tomato Sauce:

- 1 can (14 oz) crushed tomatoes
- 1 tablespoon tomato paste
- 1 teaspoon dried basil
- 1 teaspoon dried oregano
- 1 teaspoon garlic powder
- Salt and pepper, to taste

Instructions:

For the Cabbage Rolls:

Prepare Cabbage Leaves:
- Bring a large pot of water to a boil. Carefully peel off the cabbage leaves and blanch them in boiling water for 2-3 minutes until they are pliable. Remove from water and set aside to cool.

Make Filling:
- In a bowl, combine ground beef, cauliflower rice, chopped onion, minced garlic, egg, dried oregano, salt, and pepper. Mix well.

Assemble Rolls:
- Place a cabbage leaf on a flat surface. Spoon some of the beef and cauliflower rice mixture onto the center of the leaf. Fold the sides of the leaf over the filling, then roll it up to form a cabbage roll. Repeat with the remaining leaves and filling.

For the Tomato Sauce:

Prepare Sauce:

- In a bowl, mix together crushed tomatoes, tomato paste, dried basil, dried oregano, garlic powder, salt, and pepper.

Layer in Baking Dish:
- Spread a thin layer of the tomato sauce in the bottom of a baking dish.

Arrange Cabbage Rolls:
- Place the cabbage rolls in the baking dish. Pour the remaining tomato sauce over the top.

Bake:
- Cover the baking dish with foil and bake in a preheated oven at 375°F (190°C) for 45-50 minutes, or until the cabbage rolls are cooked through.

Serve:
- Once cooked, serve the Cabbage Rolls with Ground Beef and Cauliflower Rice hot, optionally garnished with fresh herbs.

This keto-friendly version of Cabbage Rolls provides all the flavors you love in a traditional recipe without the high-carb content. The combination of ground beef, cauliflower rice, and a savory tomato sauce makes for a satisfying and comforting meal.

Keto Shrimp Scampi

Ingredients:

- 1 pound large shrimp, peeled and deveined
- Salt and pepper, to taste
- 2 tablespoons olive oil
- 4 tablespoons unsalted butter
- 4 cloves garlic, minced
- 1/2 teaspoon red pepper flakes (optional, for a bit of heat)
- 1/4 cup chicken broth or dry white wine
- Zest of 1 lemon
- Juice of 1 lemon
- 2 tablespoons fresh parsley, chopped
- Zucchini noodles or cauliflower rice, for serving (optional)

Instructions:

Prepare Shrimp:
- Pat the shrimp dry with paper towels and season with salt and pepper.

Sauté Shrimp:
- In a large skillet, heat olive oil over medium-high heat. Add the shrimp to the skillet and cook for 1-2 minutes per side or until they start to turn pink. Remove the shrimp from the skillet and set aside.

Make Sauce:
- In the same skillet, add butter. Once melted, add minced garlic and red pepper flakes (if using). Sauté for about 1 minute until the garlic is fragrant.

Deglaze with Broth or Wine:
- Pour in chicken broth or white wine to deglaze the skillet, scraping any flavorful bits from the bottom. Allow the liquid to simmer for 2-3 minutes to reduce slightly.

Add Lemon Zest and Juice:
- Stir in the lemon zest and lemon juice. Mix well to combine.

Return Shrimp:
- Add the cooked shrimp back to the skillet. Toss the shrimp in the sauce until they are well-coated and heated through.

Garnish and Serve:
- Garnish the Keto Shrimp Scampi with chopped fresh parsley. Serve over zucchini noodles or cauliflower rice if desired.

Enjoy:
- Serve immediately, and enjoy your delicious and low-carb Keto Shrimp Scampi!

This Keto Shrimp Scampi is a quick and tasty dish that's perfect for a weeknight dinner. The combination of garlic, butter, and lemon creates a rich and flavorful sauce that complements the shrimp beautifully. Adjust the red pepper flakes to your spice preference, and feel free to customize the dish with your favorite low-carb side.

Bacon-wrapped Asparagus Bundles

Ingredients:

- 1 pound fresh asparagus spears, trimmed
- 8-10 slices of bacon
- Olive oil (for drizzling)
- Salt and pepper, to taste
- Garlic powder (optional)
- Lemon wedges (for serving, optional)

Instructions:

Preheat Oven:
- Preheat your oven to 400°F (200°C).

Prepare Asparagus:
- Wash and trim the tough ends from the asparagus spears. If the spears are thick, you can peel the lower part with a vegetable peeler to ensure even cooking.

Bundle Asparagus:
- Divide the asparagus into bundles, grouping 3-4 spears together.

Wrap with Bacon:
- Take a slice of bacon and wrap it around each bundle of asparagus. Place the bacon seam side down to help it stay in place.

Drizzle with Olive Oil:
- Place the bacon-wrapped asparagus bundles on a baking sheet. Drizzle with olive oil and season with salt, pepper, and garlic powder (if using).

Bake:
- Bake in the preheated oven for 20-25 minutes or until the bacon is crispy and the asparagus is tender.

Broil (Optional):
- If you want extra crispiness, you can broil the bundles for an additional 1-2 minutes under the broiler, keeping a close eye to prevent burning.

Serve:
- Remove from the oven and let them rest for a few minutes. Serve the bacon-wrapped asparagus bundles with lemon wedges on the side for a refreshing touch.

Enjoy:
- Enjoy these tasty and savory Bacon-wrapped Asparagus Bundles as a delightful appetizer or side dish!

These bacon-wrapped asparagus bundles are a crowd-pleaser and make a great addition to any meal. The combination of crispy bacon and tender asparagus creates a perfect balance of flavors. You can also experiment with additional seasonings or a sprinkle of grated Parmesan for extra flair.

Keto Meatball Subs with Almond Flour Bread

Ingredients:

For the Almond Flour Bread:

- 2 cups almond flour
- 1/4 cup coconut flour
- 1/4 cup ground flaxseed
- 1 teaspoon baking powder
- 1/2 teaspoon baking soda
- 1/2 teaspoon salt
- 4 large eggs
- 1/4 cup olive oil or melted butter
- 1/2 cup unsweetened almond milk
- 1 tablespoon apple cider vinegar

For the Meatballs:

- 1 pound ground beef or a mix of beef and pork
- 1/2 cup almond flour
- 1/4 cup grated Parmesan cheese
- 1 large egg
- 2 cloves garlic, minced
- 1 teaspoon dried oregano
- 1 teaspoon dried basil
- Salt and pepper, to taste

For Assembly:

- Low-carb marinara sauce
- Mozzarella cheese, shredded
- Fresh basil, chopped (optional)
- Red pepper flakes (optional)

Instructions:

For the Almond Flour Bread:

   Preheat Oven:
   - Preheat your oven to 350°F (175°C).

   Mix Dry Ingredients:

- In a bowl, whisk together almond flour, coconut flour, ground flaxseed, baking powder, baking soda, and salt.

Combine Wet Ingredients:
- In another bowl, beat the eggs. Add olive oil or melted butter, almond milk, and apple cider vinegar. Mix well.

Combine Mixtures:
- Add the wet ingredients to the dry ingredients and mix until well combined.

Bake Bread:
- Pour the batter into a greased or lined loaf pan. Bake in the preheated oven for 30-35 minutes or until a toothpick inserted into the center comes out clean.

Cool:
- Allow the almond flour bread to cool in the pan for 10 minutes, then transfer it to a wire rack to cool completely.

For the Meatballs:

Preheat Oven:
- Increase the oven temperature to 400°F (200°C).

Mix Meatball Ingredients:
- In a bowl, combine ground beef, almond flour, grated Parmesan, egg, minced garlic, dried oregano, dried basil, salt, and pepper. Mix until well combined.

Form Meatballs:
- Shape the mixture into meatballs and place them on a baking sheet lined with parchment paper.

Bake Meatballs:
- Bake in the preheated oven for 15-20 minutes or until the meatballs are cooked through.

For Assembly:

Slice Almond Flour Bread:
- Once cooled, slice the almond flour bread into sub-sized pieces.

Assemble Subs:
- Place meatballs on the sliced almond flour bread. Top with low-carb marinara sauce and shredded mozzarella cheese.

Broil:
- Place the assembled subs under the broiler for a few minutes until the cheese is melted and bubbly.

Garnish and Serve:
- Garnish with chopped fresh basil and red pepper flakes if desired. Serve your Keto Meatball Subs and enjoy!

These Keto Meatball Subs with Almond Flour Bread provide the classic flavors of a meatball sub without the high-carb content. The almond flour bread is a satisfying and tasty substitute, and the meatballs are flavorful and tender. Customize with your favorite low-carb toppings and enjoy a delicious keto-friendly meal.

Creamy Garlic Parmesan Brussels Sprouts

Ingredients:

- 1 pound Brussels sprouts, trimmed and halved
- 2 tablespoons butter
- 4 cloves garlic, minced
- 1/2 cup heavy cream
- 1/2 cup grated Parmesan cheese
- Salt and pepper, to taste
- Fresh parsley, chopped (for garnish, optional)

Instructions:

Prepare Brussels Sprouts:
- Trim the ends of the Brussels sprouts and cut them in half.

Steam Brussels Sprouts:
- Steam or boil the Brussels sprouts until they are just tender. This usually takes about 5-7 minutes. Drain and set aside.

Sauté Garlic:
- In a large skillet, melt the butter over medium heat. Add minced garlic and sauté for 1-2 minutes until fragrant.

Add Brussels Sprouts:
- Add the steamed Brussels sprouts to the skillet, tossing them in the garlic butter to coat.

Pour Heavy Cream:
- Pour the heavy cream over the Brussels sprouts and stir to combine.

Add Parmesan Cheese:
- Sprinkle the grated Parmesan cheese over the Brussels sprouts. Stir continuously until the cheese is melted and the sauce is creamy.

Season:
- Season the dish with salt and pepper to taste. Adjust the seasoning according to your preference.

Garnish and Serve:
- Garnish with fresh chopped parsley if desired.

Serve:
- Transfer the Creamy Garlic Parmesan Brussels Sprouts to a serving dish and serve hot.

This Creamy Garlic Parmesan Brussels Sprouts recipe offers a perfect balance of rich and creamy flavors with the nutty taste of Parmesan. It's a delightful side dish that pairs well with various main courses. Adjust the level of garlic, Parmesan, and seasoning to suit your taste preferences. Enjoy!

Keto Beef and Broccoli Stir-Fry

Ingredients:

For the Beef Marinade:

- 1 pound flank steak, thinly sliced against the grain
- 2 tablespoons soy sauce or tamari (for gluten-free option)
- 1 tablespoon dry sherry or rice wine
- 1 tablespoon sesame oil
- 1 tablespoon erythritol or your preferred keto-friendly sweetener
- 1 teaspoon minced garlic
- 1 teaspoon minced ginger
- 1 tablespoon olive oil (for cooking)

For the Stir-Fry Sauce:

- 1/4 cup soy sauce or tamari
- 2 tablespoons oyster sauce
- 1 tablespoon dry sherry or rice wine
- 1 tablespoon sesame oil
- 1 tablespoon erythritol or your preferred keto-friendly sweetener
- 1 teaspoon xanthan gum (optional, for thickening)

For the Stir-Fry:

- 1 pound broccoli, cut into small florets
- 2 tablespoons olive oil (for cooking)
- Sesame seeds, for garnish (optional)
- Green onions, sliced, for garnish (optional)
- Cauliflower rice, for serving (optional)

Instructions:

1. Marinate the Beef:

   In a bowl, combine the thinly sliced flank steak with soy sauce, dry sherry or rice wine, sesame oil, erythritol, minced garlic, and minced ginger.
   Let the beef marinate for at least 15-20 minutes.

2. Prepare the Stir-Fry Sauce:

In a small bowl, whisk together soy sauce or tamari, oyster sauce, dry sherry or rice wine, sesame oil, and erythritol.

If you prefer a thicker sauce, you can add xanthan gum and whisk until well combined.

3. Cook the Broccoli:

Steam or blanch the broccoli florets until they are just tender, about 2-3 minutes.
Drain and set aside.

4. Stir-Fry:

Heat 1 tablespoon of olive oil in a large wok or skillet over medium-high heat.
Add the marinated beef to the hot wok and stir-fry for 2-3 minutes or until the beef is browned and cooked to your liking.
Remove the beef from the wok and set it aside.

5. Cook the Broccoli with Sauce:

In the same wok, add another 2 tablespoons of olive oil.
Add the steamed broccoli to the wok and stir-fry for 2-3 minutes.
Pour the stir-fry sauce over the broccoli and continue to cook for an additional 1-2 minutes, allowing the sauce to thicken slightly.

6. Combine Beef and Broccoli:

Return the cooked beef to the wok and toss it with the broccoli until everything is well-coated in the sauce.
Cook for an additional 1-2 minutes to heat through.

7. Serve:

Serve the Keto Beef and Broccoli Stir-Fry over cauliflower rice if desired.
Garnish with sesame seeds and sliced green onions, if you like.

Enjoy your delicious Keto Beef and Broccoli Stir-Fry! Adjust the seasoning and spice levels according to your taste preferences. It's a satisfying low-carb dish that captures the essence of the classic stir-fry.

Spinach and Feta Stuffed Chicken Breast

Ingredients:

- 4 boneless, skinless chicken breasts
- Salt and pepper, to taste
- 2 tablespoons olive oil

For the Spinach and Feta Filling:

- 2 cups fresh spinach, chopped
- 1/2 cup feta cheese, crumbled
- 1/4 cup cream cheese
- 2 cloves garlic, minced
- 1 tablespoon olive oil
- Salt and pepper, to taste

For Seasoning the Chicken:

- 1 teaspoon paprika
- 1 teaspoon dried oregano
- 1 teaspoon garlic powder

Instructions:

1. Prepare the Spinach and Feta Filling:

    In a skillet, heat 1 tablespoon of olive oil over medium heat.
    Add minced garlic and sauté for 1-2 minutes until fragrant.
    Add chopped spinach and cook until wilted.
    Transfer the spinach to a bowl and let it cool.
    Once cooled, mix in crumbled feta and cream cheese. Season with salt and pepper to taste.

2. Butterfly and Season the Chicken:

    Preheat your oven to 375°F (190°C).
    Butterfly each chicken breast by slicing horizontally, keeping one edge intact, to create a pocket for the filling.
    Season the inside of each chicken breast with salt, pepper, paprika, dried oregano, and garlic powder.

3. Stuff the Chicken:

> Spoon the spinach and feta filling into the pocket of each chicken breast, pressing it down gently.
> Secure the opening with toothpicks to hold the filling in place.

4. Sear the Chicken:

> Heat 2 tablespoons of olive oil in an oven-safe skillet over medium-high heat.
> Sear the stuffed chicken breasts for 2-3 minutes on each side until golden brown.

5. Finish in the Oven:

> Transfer the skillet to the preheated oven.
> Bake for 20-25 minutes or until the chicken reaches an internal temperature of 165°F (74°C) and the juices run clear.

6. Rest and Serve:

> Allow the Spinach and Feta Stuffed Chicken Breast to rest for a few minutes before slicing.
> Remove the toothpicks before serving.

7. Serve:

> Serve the stuffed chicken breasts with your favorite side dishes.
> Enjoy your delicious Spinach and Feta Stuffed Chicken!

This Spinach and Feta Stuffed Chicken Breast is a flavorful and satisfying dish. The combination of creamy feta and spinach adds a burst of flavor to the tender chicken. It's a great option for a special dinner or a meal to impress guests.

Keto Taco Salad with Ground Turkey

Ingredients:

For the Ground Turkey:

- 1 pound ground turkey
- 1 tablespoon olive oil
- 1 packet taco seasoning (make sure it's keto-friendly or use homemade seasoning)

For the Salad:

- 8 cups shredded lettuce (e.g., iceberg or romaine)
- 1 cup cherry tomatoes, halved
- 1 cup shredded cheddar cheese
- 1/2 cup diced red onion
- 1/4 cup sliced black olives (optional)
- 1 avocado, sliced
- Fresh cilantro, chopped (for garnish)

For the Dressing:

- 1/2 cup sour cream
- 2 tablespoons mayonnaise
- 1 tablespoon lime juice
- 1 teaspoon taco seasoning

Instructions:

For the Ground Turkey:

Cook Turkey:
- In a skillet, heat olive oil over medium heat. Add ground turkey and cook until browned, breaking it apart with a spatula.

Season with Taco Seasoning:
- Sprinkle taco seasoning over the cooked turkey. Follow the package instructions or adjust the seasoning to your taste. Cook for an additional 2-3 minutes, allowing the flavors to meld. Set aside.

For the Salad:

Prepare Vegetables:

- In a large bowl, combine shredded lettuce, cherry tomatoes, shredded cheddar cheese, diced red onion, sliced black olives (if using), and avocado slices.

For the Dressing:

Make Dressing:
- In a small bowl, whisk together sour cream, mayonnaise, lime juice, and taco seasoning until well combined.

Assemble the Keto Taco Salad:

Layer Salad:
- On individual plates or in a large serving bowl, layer the seasoned ground turkey over the salad mixture.

Drizzle with Dressing:
- Drizzle the dressing over the salad.

Garnish:
- Garnish with fresh cilantro.

Serve:
- Serve immediately and enjoy your delicious Keto Taco Salad with Ground Turkey!

This Keto Taco Salad with Ground Turkey is not only low in carbs but also packed with flavor and texture. The combination of seasoned ground turkey, fresh vegetables, and a creamy dressing creates a satisfying and satisfying meal. Feel free to customize the salad with your favorite keto-friendly toppings and enjoy a tasty and satisfying dish.

Sausage and Egg Breakfast Casserole

Ingredients:

- 1 pound breakfast sausage (pork or turkey), cooked and crumbled
- 8 large eggs
- 1 cup milk (or a non-dairy alternative)
- 1 teaspoon Dijon mustard
- 1/2 teaspoon salt
- 1/4 teaspoon black pepper
- 2 cups shredded cheddar cheese
- 4 cups cubed bread (such as French bread or whole wheat bread)
- 1/2 cup diced bell peppers (optional)
- 1/2 cup diced onions (optional)
- 1/4 cup chopped fresh parsley (optional)
- Cooking spray or butter (for greasing the baking dish)

Instructions:

Preheat Oven:
- Preheat your oven to 350°F (175°C).

Prepare Baking Dish:
- Grease a 9x13-inch baking dish with cooking spray or butter.

Layer Ingredients:
- In the prepared baking dish, layer the cubed bread, cooked and crumbled sausage, shredded cheddar cheese, and any optional vegetables (bell peppers, onions, parsley).

Whisk Egg Mixture:
- In a bowl, whisk together eggs, milk, Dijon mustard, salt, and black pepper until well combined.

Pour Egg Mixture:
- Pour the egg mixture evenly over the layered ingredients in the baking dish.

Press Down:
- Gently press down on the ingredients with a spatula to ensure the bread absorbs the egg mixture.

Rest and Soak:
- Let the casserole sit for about 15 minutes to allow the bread to soak up the egg mixture.

Bake:

- Bake in the preheated oven for 45-50 minutes or until the top is golden brown, and the eggs are set.

Cool and Serve:
- Allow the Sausage and Egg Breakfast Casserole to cool for a few minutes before slicing and serving.

Optional Garnish:
- Garnish with additional chopped fresh parsley if desired.

Serve:
- Serve warm and enjoy your delicious Sausage and Egg Breakfast Casserole!

This breakfast casserole is versatile, and you can customize it with your favorite ingredients. It's a great make-ahead dish for busy mornings or brunch gatherings. Feel free to experiment with different cheeses, herbs, or vegetables to suit your taste preferences.

Keto Broccoli Cheddar Soup

Ingredients:

- 4 cups fresh broccoli florets
- 1/4 cup unsalted butter
- 1/4 cup almond flour
- 1 small onion, finely chopped
- 2 cloves garlic, minced
- 4 cups chicken or vegetable broth
- 1 cup heavy cream
- 2 cups shredded sharp cheddar cheese
- Salt and pepper, to taste
- Pinch of nutmeg (optional, for extra flavor)

Instructions:

Cook Broccoli:
- Steam or boil the broccoli florets until they are tender. Set aside.

Make Roux:
- In a large pot, melt the butter over medium heat. Add the almond flour and stir continuously to form a roux. Cook for 2-3 minutes until it becomes a light golden color.

Sauté Onion and Garlic:
- Add the chopped onion and minced garlic to the pot. Sauté for 2-3 minutes until the onions are softened.

Add Broth:
- Gradually whisk in the chicken or vegetable broth, ensuring that there are no lumps. Bring the mixture to a simmer.

Add Broccoli:
- Add the cooked broccoli to the pot and let it simmer for an additional 5 minutes.

Blend Soup (Optional):
- If you prefer a smoother texture, you can use an immersion blender to partially blend the soup. Leave some broccoli pieces for texture.

Add Heavy Cream:
- Pour in the heavy cream and stir to combine.

Add Cheddar Cheese:
- Gradually add the shredded cheddar cheese, stirring continuously until the cheese is melted and the soup is smooth.

Season:
- Season the soup with salt, pepper, and a pinch of nutmeg if desired. Adjust the seasoning according to your taste.

Simmer:
- Let the soup simmer for an additional 5-10 minutes to allow the flavors to meld.

Serve:
- Ladle the Keto Broccoli Cheddar Soup into bowls and serve hot.

This Keto Broccoli Cheddar Soup is rich, creamy, and low in carbs, making it a perfect comfort food for those following a ketogenic lifestyle. Enjoy it on its own or with a side salad for a satisfying meal. Feel free to customize the soup with additional seasonings or garnishes as per your preference.

Avocado and Bacon Stuffed Mushrooms

Ingredients:

- 12 large mushrooms, cleaned and stems removed
- 1 ripe avocado, peeled and diced
- 4 slices bacon, cooked and crumbled
- 1/4 cup red onion, finely diced
- 1 tablespoon fresh cilantro, chopped
- 1 tablespoon lime or lemon juice
- Salt and pepper, to taste
- 1/2 cup shredded cheese (cheddar or mozzarella), optional
- Fresh parsley or additional cilantro for garnish, optional

Instructions:

Preheat Oven:
- Preheat your oven to 375°F (190°C).

Prepare Mushrooms:
- Clean the mushrooms and remove the stems. Place the mushroom caps on a baking sheet, cap side down.

Prepare Filling:
- In a bowl, combine diced avocado, crumbled bacon, red onion, cilantro, lime or lemon juice, salt, and pepper. Mix well.

Stuff Mushrooms:
- Spoon the avocado and bacon mixture into each mushroom cap, pressing down gently to pack the filling.

Optional Cheese Topping:
- If you desire, sprinkle shredded cheese on top of each stuffed mushroom.

Bake:
- Bake in the preheated oven for 15-20 minutes or until the mushrooms are tender and the filling is heated through.

Garnish and Serve:
- If desired, garnish the stuffed mushrooms with fresh parsley or additional cilantro.

Serve:
- Serve the Avocado and Bacon Stuffed Mushrooms warm as a delightful appetizer.

These stuffed mushrooms are a delicious combination of creamy avocado, smoky bacon, and savory mushrooms. The lime or lemon juice adds a bright citrusy flavor to balance the richness. Whether you serve them at a party or enjoy them as a snack, these stuffed mushrooms are sure to be a hit.

Keto Cauliflower Mac and Cheese

Ingredients:

- 1 large head cauliflower, cut into florets
- 2 tablespoons butter
- 2 tablespoons almond flour
- 1 1/2 cups heavy cream
- 2 cups shredded sharp cheddar cheese
- 1 cup shredded mozzarella cheese
- 1/2 cup grated Parmesan cheese
- 1 teaspoon Dijon mustard
- Salt and pepper, to taste
- 1/4 teaspoon garlic powder (optional)
- Chopped fresh parsley, for garnish (optional)
- Crispy bacon bits, for topping (optional)

Instructions:

Preheat Oven:
- Preheat your oven to 375°F (190°C).

Steam Cauliflower:
- Steam the cauliflower florets until they are just tender. Drain and set aside.

Make Cheese Sauce:
- In a large saucepan, melt the butter over medium heat. Add almond flour and whisk continuously for 1-2 minutes to create a roux.

Add Heavy Cream:
- Gradually pour in the heavy cream, whisking constantly to avoid lumps.

Melt Cheeses:
- Add the shredded cheddar, mozzarella, and grated Parmesan cheese to the sauce. Stir until the cheeses are melted and the sauce is smooth.

Season:
- Stir in Dijon mustard and season the sauce with salt, pepper, and garlic powder (if using). Adjust the seasoning according to your taste.

Combine with Cauliflower:
- Add the steamed cauliflower to the cheese sauce, gently folding to coat the cauliflower with the sauce.

Transfer to Baking Dish:
- Transfer the cauliflower and cheese mixture to a greased baking dish.

Bake:

- Bake in the preheated oven for 20-25 minutes or until the top is golden and bubbly.

Optional Toppings:
- If desired, garnish with chopped fresh parsley and crispy bacon bits before serving.

Serve:
- Serve the Keto Cauliflower Mac and Cheese warm as a delicious and satisfying low-carb alternative.

This Keto Cauliflower Mac and Cheese is a rich and cheesy dish that's sure to satisfy your comfort food cravings while keeping it low-carb. Feel free to customize it with your favorite keto-friendly toppings or additional seasonings. Enjoy!

Grilled Lemon Herb Chicken Thighs

Ingredients:

- 4-6 bone-in, skin-on chicken thighs
- 2 lemons, juiced and zested
- 3 tablespoons olive oil
- 2 cloves garlic, minced
- 1 teaspoon dried oregano
- 1 teaspoon dried thyme
- 1 teaspoon dried rosemary
- Salt and pepper, to taste
- Fresh parsley, chopped (for garnish, optional)

Instructions:

Prepare Marinade:
- In a bowl, whisk together the lemon juice, lemon zest, olive oil, minced garlic, dried oregano, dried thyme, dried rosemary, salt, and pepper.

Marinate Chicken:
- Place the chicken thighs in a large resealable plastic bag or a shallow dish. Pour the marinade over the chicken, ensuring each piece is well coated. Seal the bag or cover the dish and refrigerate for at least 30 minutes, or ideally, marinate overnight for more flavor.

Preheat Grill:
- Preheat your grill to medium-high heat.

Grill Chicken:
- Remove the chicken from the marinade and let any excess drip off. Place the chicken thighs on the preheated grill, skin side down. Grill for about 5-7 minutes per side or until the internal temperature reaches 165°F (74°C) and the skin is crispy and golden brown.

Baste with Marinade (Optional):
- If you'd like, you can baste the chicken with some of the marinade during the last few minutes of grilling for added flavor.

Rest and Garnish:
- Remove the chicken thighs from the grill and let them rest for a few minutes before serving. Garnish with chopped fresh parsley if desired.

Serve:
- Serve the Grilled Lemon Herb Chicken Thighs hot with your favorite side dishes.

This Grilled Lemon Herb Chicken Thighs recipe provides a perfect balance of citrusy and herby flavors. The combination of lemon and herbs complements the smoky grill flavor, making it a delightful and savory dish. Enjoy it with a fresh salad, grilled vegetables, or your preferred sides for a complete meal.

Keto Egg Drop Soup

Ingredients:

- 4 cups chicken broth (homemade or store-bought, preferably low sodium)
- 2 large eggs
- 1 tablespoon soy sauce or tamari (for gluten-free option)
- 1 teaspoon sesame oil
- 1/4 teaspoon ground white pepper
- 2 green onions, thinly sliced (for garnish)
- Fresh cilantro, chopped (for garnish, optional)

Instructions:

Heat Chicken Broth:
- In a medium-sized saucepan, heat the chicken broth over medium-high heat until it comes to a gentle simmer.

Season with Soy Sauce and Sesame Oil:
- Stir in the soy sauce (or tamari), sesame oil, and ground white pepper. Adjust the seasoning to your taste.

Whisk Eggs:
- In a small bowl, whisk the eggs until well beaten.

Create Egg Ribbons:
- Once the broth is simmering, use a fork or chopsticks to stir the broth in a circular motion. While stirring, slowly pour the beaten eggs into the moving broth. The eggs will cook instantly, creating silky ribbons.

Garnish and Serve:
- Add sliced green onions and chopped cilantro (if using) to the soup. Stir gently.

Adjust Seasoning:
- Taste the soup and adjust the seasoning if necessary.

Serve Warm:
- Ladle the Keto Egg Drop Soup into bowls and serve warm.

This Keto Egg Drop Soup is not only low in carbs but also a comforting and quick dish to prepare. It's a great way to enjoy a warm and savory bowl of soup while staying within your keto lifestyle. Feel free to customize it with additional ingredients like mushrooms or spinach if you'd like. Enjoy!

Cauliflower Fried Rice

Ingredients:

- 1 medium-sized cauliflower, grated or finely chopped (or use pre-riced cauliflower)
- 2 tablespoons sesame oil
- 2 cloves garlic, minced
- 1 tablespoon ginger, minced
- 1 cup mixed vegetables (e.g., peas, carrots, corn)
- 2 green onions, thinly sliced
- 2 eggs, beaten
- 3 tablespoons soy sauce or tamari (for gluten-free option)
- 1 tablespoon rice vinegar
- Salt and pepper, to taste
- Sesame seeds and chopped cilantro for garnish (optional)

Instructions:

Prepare Cauliflower Rice:
- Grate the cauliflower using a box grater or pulse it in a food processor until it resembles rice-sized pieces. Set aside.

Cook Vegetables:
- In a large skillet or wok, heat sesame oil over medium-high heat. Add minced garlic and ginger, sautéing for about 30 seconds until fragrant.
- Add mixed vegetables to the skillet and cook until they are tender, about 3-4 minutes.

Add Cauliflower Rice:
- Push the vegetables to one side of the skillet and add the riced cauliflower. Stir to combine with the vegetables.

Create Well for Eggs:
- Create a well in the center of the cauliflower and vegetable mixture. Pour beaten eggs into the well.

Scramble Eggs:
- Allow the eggs to set for a moment, then scramble them with a spatula until fully cooked.

Combine and Season:
- Mix the cooked eggs with the cauliflower and vegetables. Add soy sauce (or tamari) and rice vinegar. Stir well to combine.

- Season with salt and pepper to taste. Adjust soy sauce or tamari according to your preference.

Garnish and Serve:
- Garnish the Cauliflower Fried Rice with sliced green onions, sesame seeds, and chopped cilantro if desired.

Serve Warm:
- Serve the Cauliflower Fried Rice warm as a delicious and low-carb alternative to traditional fried rice.

This Cauliflower Fried Rice is a versatile dish that can be customized with your favorite protein, such as chicken, shrimp, or tofu. It's a flavorful and satisfying option for those looking to reduce their carb intake while still enjoying a classic Asian-inspired dish.

Keto Tuna Salad Lettuce Wraps

Ingredients:

- 1 can (5 ounces) tuna, drained
- 2 tablespoons mayonnaise
- 1 tablespoon Dijon mustard
- 1 celery stalk, finely chopped
- 2 green onions, finely sliced
- Salt and pepper, to taste
- Butter lettuce leaves (or any lettuce with large, flexible leaves)
- Avocado slices (optional, for topping)
- Cucumber slices (optional, for topping)
- Cherry tomatoes (optional, for topping)
- Lemon wedges (for serving)

Instructions:

Prepare Tuna Salad:
- In a bowl, combine drained tuna, mayonnaise, Dijon mustard, chopped celery, and sliced green onions. Mix well.

Season:
- Season the tuna salad with salt and pepper to taste. Adjust the seasoning according to your preference.

Assemble Lettuce Wraps:
- Spoon the tuna salad onto individual butter lettuce leaves, creating a bed of salad.

Add Toppings (Optional):
- Top each lettuce wrap with avocado slices, cucumber slices, and cherry tomatoes if desired.

Serve with Lemon Wedges:
- Serve the Keto Tuna Salad Lettuce Wraps with lemon wedges on the side.

Enjoy:
- Enjoy the lettuce wraps as a light and satisfying keto-friendly meal.

These Keto Tuna Salad Lettuce Wraps are not only low in carbs but also high in protein and healthy fats. You can customize the toppings based on your preferences, adding extra veggies for freshness and crunch. It's a quick and easy option for a nutritious lunch or snack without the need for bread or traditional wraps.

Cheesy Bacon-Wrapped Jalapeño Poppers

Ingredients:

- 12 large jalapeño peppers
- 8 ounces cream cheese, softened
- 1 cup shredded cheddar cheese
- 1 teaspoon garlic powder
- 1/2 teaspoon onion powder
- Salt and pepper, to taste
- 12 slices of bacon, cut in half
- Toothpicks

Instructions:

Preheat Oven:
- Preheat your oven to 400°F (200°C). Line a baking sheet with parchment paper.

Prepare Jalapeños:
- Cut jalapeños in half lengthwise, removing seeds and membranes. Wear gloves or wash hands thoroughly after handling jalapeños.

Prepare Filling:
- In a bowl, mix softened cream cheese, shredded cheddar cheese, garlic powder, onion powder, salt, and pepper until well combined.

Fill Jalapeños:
- Spoon the cream cheese mixture into each jalapeño half, spreading it evenly.

Wrap with Bacon:
- Wrap each cream cheese-filled jalapeño half with a half-slice of bacon, securing it with a toothpick.

Bake:
- Place the bacon-wrapped jalapeños on the prepared baking sheet. Bake in the preheated oven for 20-25 minutes or until the bacon is crispy.

Broil (Optional):
- If the bacon needs additional crisping, you can broil the jalapeño poppers for 1-2 minutes, watching carefully to prevent burning.

Serve:
- Remove the toothpicks before serving. Serve the Cheesy Bacon-Wrapped Jalapeño Poppers warm.

These Cheesy Bacon-Wrapped Jalapeño Poppers are a crowd-pleasing appetizer that combines the heat of jalapeños with the creaminess of cheese and the savory goodness of bacon. They are perfect for entertaining or as a tasty snack. Adjust the amount of jalapeños and the level of spice to suit your taste preferences. Enjoy!

Keto Buffalo Chicken Dip

Ingredients:

- 2 cups cooked chicken, shredded (rotisserie chicken works well)
- 8 ounces cream cheese, softened
- 1/2 cup mayonnaise
- 1/2 cup sour cream
- 1/2 cup buffalo sauce (adjust to taste)
- 1 teaspoon garlic powder
- 1 teaspoon onion powder
- 1/2 teaspoon dried dill (optional)
- 1/2 cup shredded cheddar cheese
- 1/2 cup shredded mozzarella cheese
- Green onions, chopped (for garnish, optional)
- Celery sticks or low-carb crackers (for serving)

Instructions:

Preheat Oven:
- Preheat your oven to 350°F (175°C).

Mix Cream Cheese Mixture:
- In a large mixing bowl, combine softened cream cheese, mayonnaise, sour cream, buffalo sauce, garlic powder, onion powder, and dried dill. Mix until well combined.

Add Chicken and Cheese:
- Stir in the shredded chicken, cheddar cheese, and mozzarella cheese, mixing until all ingredients are evenly incorporated.

Transfer to Baking Dish:
- Transfer the mixture to a baking dish, spreading it out evenly.

Bake:
- Bake in the preheated oven for 20-25 minutes or until the dip is hot and bubbly, and the top is golden brown.

Garnish and Serve:
- Remove from the oven and garnish with chopped green onions if desired.

Serve Warm:
- Serve the Keto Buffalo Chicken Dip warm with celery sticks or low-carb crackers for dipping.

This Keto Buffalo Chicken Dip is a crowd-pleaser and a great option for those following a low-carb or keto lifestyle. The combination of creamy textures, spicy buffalo sauce, and shredded chicken creates a flavorful and satisfying appetizer. Adjust the level of heat by adding more or less buffalo sauce according to your preference. Enjoy!

Spaghetti Squash with Pesto and Cherry Tomatoes

Ingredients:

- 1 medium-sized spaghetti squash
- 1 cup cherry tomatoes, halved
- 1/4 cup pine nuts, toasted
- 1/2 cup freshly grated Parmesan cheese
- Fresh basil leaves, for garnish

For the Pesto:

- 2 cups fresh basil leaves
- 1/2 cup freshly grated Parmesan cheese
- 1/2 cup extra-virgin olive oil
- 1/4 cup pine nuts, toasted
- 2 cloves garlic, peeled
- Salt and pepper, to taste

Instructions:

Prepare the Spaghetti Squash:
- Preheat the oven to 375°F (190°C). Cut the spaghetti squash in half lengthwise and scoop out the seeds. Place the squash halves, cut side down, on a baking sheet. Roast in the preheated oven for about 40-50 minutes or until the squash is tender and the strands easily come apart with a fork.

Make the Pesto:
- In a food processor, combine fresh basil, grated Parmesan cheese, pine nuts, garlic, salt, and pepper. Pulse until the ingredients are finely chopped. With the processor running, slowly drizzle in the olive oil until the pesto reaches your desired consistency. Adjust salt and pepper to taste.

Scrape Spaghetti Squash:
- Once the spaghetti squash is cooked, use a fork to scrape the strands into a large bowl.

Toss with Pesto and Tomatoes:
- Add the prepared pesto to the spaghetti squash strands and toss until well coated. Add halved cherry tomatoes and toss gently.

Toast Pine Nuts:

- In a dry skillet over medium heat, toast the pine nuts until they are golden brown. Watch them carefully to prevent burning.

Serve:
- Serve the Spaghetti Squash with Pesto and Cherry Tomatoes in individual bowls. Top with toasted pine nuts, freshly grated Parmesan cheese, and garnish with fresh basil leaves.

This Spaghetti Squash with Pesto and Cherry Tomatoes is a flavorful and satisfying dish that's packed with the vibrant flavors of fresh basil and sweet cherry tomatoes. It's a great way to enjoy a low-carb, gluten-free alternative to traditional pasta. Feel free to customize the dish with additional ingredients such as grilled chicken or shrimp for added protein. Enjoy!

Keto Chicken Zoodle Soup

Ingredients:

- 2 tablespoons olive oil
- 1 onion, finely chopped
- 2 carrots, peeled and sliced
- 2 celery stalks, sliced
- 3 cloves garlic, minced
- 6 cups chicken broth (homemade or store-bought, preferably low sodium)
- 2 cups cooked chicken, shredded (rotisserie chicken works well)
- 2 medium zucchini, spiralized into zoodles
- 1 teaspoon dried thyme
- 1 teaspoon dried oregano
- Salt and pepper, to taste
- Fresh parsley, chopped (for garnish, optional)
- Lemon wedges (for serving, optional)

Instructions:

Sauté Vegetables:
- In a large pot, heat olive oil over medium heat. Add chopped onion, sliced carrots, and sliced celery. Sauté until the vegetables are softened, about 5 minutes.

Add Garlic:
- Add minced garlic to the pot and sauté for an additional 1-2 minutes until fragrant.

Pour in Chicken Broth:
- Pour in the chicken broth, bringing the mixture to a simmer.

Season and Add Chicken:
- Season the soup with dried thyme, dried oregano, salt, and pepper. Add the shredded cooked chicken to the pot and let it simmer for 10-15 minutes to allow the flavors to meld.

Add Zucchini Noodles:
- Add the spiralized zucchini noodles to the pot. Simmer for an additional 5-7 minutes until the zoodles are just tender.

Adjust Seasoning:
- Taste the soup and adjust the seasoning if necessary.

Garnish and Serve:

- Ladle the Keto Chicken Zoodle Soup into bowls. Garnish with fresh chopped parsley and serve with lemon wedges if desired.

This Keto Chicken Zoodle Soup is a light, flavorful, and satisfying option for those following a low-carb lifestyle. The zucchini noodles add a refreshing twist to the classic chicken noodle soup. Feel free to customize the soup with additional vegetables or herbs based on your preferences. Enjoy!

Baked Parmesan Crusted Salmon

Ingredients:

- 4 salmon fillets (about 6 ounces each)
- 1/2 cup grated Parmesan cheese
- 1/4 cup breadcrumbs (or almond flour for a low-carb option)
- 2 tablespoons melted butter
- 1 tablespoon Dijon mustard
- 1 tablespoon chopped fresh parsley
- 1 teaspoon garlic powder
- 1 teaspoon dried oregano
- Salt and pepper, to taste
- Lemon wedges (for serving)

Instructions:

Preheat Oven:
- Preheat your oven to 400°F (200°C). Line a baking sheet with parchment paper or lightly grease it.

Prepare Parmesan Mixture:
- In a bowl, combine grated Parmesan cheese, breadcrumbs (or almond flour), melted butter, Dijon mustard, chopped parsley, garlic powder, dried oregano, salt, and pepper. Mix well until it forms a crumbly mixture.

Coat Salmon Fillets:
- Place the salmon fillets on the prepared baking sheet. Press the Parmesan mixture onto the top of each salmon fillet, creating a crust.

Bake:
- Bake in the preheated oven for 12-15 minutes or until the salmon is cooked through and the crust is golden brown.

Serve:
- Remove from the oven and let the Baked Parmesan Crusted Salmon rest for a few minutes. Serve warm with lemon wedges on the side.

Optional Broil (for extra crispiness):
- If you prefer a crispier crust, you can broil the salmon for an additional 1-2 minutes, watching carefully to prevent burning.

Garnish and Enjoy:
- Garnish with additional chopped parsley if desired. Serve the Baked Parmesan Crusted Salmon with your favorite side dishes.

This Baked Parmesan Crusted Salmon is a quick and flavorful way to enjoy salmon with a crispy, cheesy coating. It's a versatile dish that pairs well with a variety of sides such as roasted vegetables, salad, or quinoa. Adjust the seasonings to your liking and enjoy a delicious and nutritious meal.

Keto Avocado Chocolate Pudding

Ingredients:

- 2 ripe avocados, peeled and pitted
- 1/4 cup unsweetened cocoa powder
- 1/4 cup almond milk (or any low-carb milk alternative)
- 1/4 cup powdered erythritol or any keto-friendly sweetener, adjust to taste
- 1 teaspoon vanilla extract
- Pinch of salt

Instructions:

Blend Avocados:
- In a blender or food processor, combine the ripe avocados, cocoa powder, almond milk, powdered erythritol, vanilla extract, and a pinch of salt.

Blend until Smooth:
- Blend the ingredients until smooth and creamy. Stop and scrape down the sides of the blender or processor as needed.

Adjust Sweetness:
- Taste the pudding and adjust the sweetness by adding more powdered erythritol if necessary.

Chill:
- Transfer the keto avocado chocolate pudding to serving bowls or glasses. Cover and refrigerate for at least 1-2 hours to allow it to chill and thicken.

Serve:
- Serve the Keto Avocado Chocolate Pudding chilled. You can top it with whipped cream or a sprinkle of cocoa powder if desired.

Optional Garnish:
- Garnish with fresh berries or a few chopped nuts for added texture and flavor.

This Keto Avocado Chocolate Pudding is a delightful and guilt-free treat that satisfies your chocolate cravings while staying low in carbs. The creamy texture of avocados provides a luxurious consistency to the pudding, and the cocoa powder adds that rich chocolate flavor. Enjoy this keto-friendly dessert as part of your low-carb lifestyle.

Low-Carb Zucchini Bread

Ingredients:

- 2 cups grated zucchini (about 2 medium-sized zucchinis)
- 2 1/2 cups almond flour
- 1/2 cup coconut flour
- 1/2 cup unsweetened shredded coconut
- 1/2 cup granulated erythritol or any keto-friendly sweetener
- 1 teaspoon baking powder
- 1/2 teaspoon baking soda
- 1/2 teaspoon salt
- 1 teaspoon ground cinnamon
- 1/2 teaspoon ground nutmeg
- 4 large eggs
- 1/2 cup unsalted butter, melted
- 1 teaspoon vanilla extract
- 1/2 cup chopped nuts (walnuts or pecans), optional

Instructions:

Preheat Oven:
- Preheat your oven to 350°F (175°C). Grease or line a loaf pan with parchment paper.

Grate Zucchini:
- Grate the zucchinis using a box grater. Place the grated zucchini in a clean kitchen towel and squeeze out excess moisture.

Combine Dry Ingredients:
- In a large mixing bowl, combine almond flour, coconut flour, shredded coconut, erythritol, baking powder, baking soda, salt, ground cinnamon, and ground nutmeg. Mix well.

Add Wet Ingredients:
- Add the grated zucchini, eggs, melted butter, and vanilla extract to the dry ingredients. Mix until well combined.

Fold in Nuts (Optional):
- If you're using nuts, fold in the chopped nuts into the batter.

Pour into Pan:
- Pour the batter into the prepared loaf pan, spreading it evenly.

Bake:

- Bake in the preheated oven for 50-60 minutes or until a toothpick inserted into the center comes out clean.

Cool:
- Allow the low-carb zucchini bread to cool in the pan for 10-15 minutes, then transfer it to a wire rack to cool completely.

Slice and Serve:
- Once cooled, slice and serve the Low-Carb Zucchini Bread. Enjoy!

This Low-Carb Zucchini Bread is a moist and flavorful treat that's perfect for those following a keto or low-carb diet. The combination of almond flour, coconut flour, and zucchini creates a satisfying bread that's both delicious and nutritious. Feel free to customize the recipe by adding your favorite low-carb mix-ins, such as sugar-free chocolate chips or berries.

Keto Cauliflower Hummus

Ingredients:

- 4 cups cauliflower florets
- 2 cloves garlic, minced
- 1/4 cup tahini
- 1/4 cup olive oil
- 2 tablespoons lemon juice
- 1/2 teaspoon ground cumin
- 1/2 teaspoon ground coriander
- Salt and pepper, to taste
- 2 tablespoons chopped fresh parsley (for garnish)
- Extra olive oil (for drizzling, optional)

Instructions:

Steam Cauliflower:
- Steam the cauliflower florets until they are very tender. This can be done using a steamer basket on the stove or by microwaving the cauliflower with a bit of water.

Blend Ingredients:
- In a food processor, combine the steamed cauliflower, minced garlic, tahini, olive oil, lemon juice, ground cumin, and ground coriander. Blend until smooth and creamy.

Season:
- Season the cauliflower hummus with salt and pepper, adjusting to your taste preferences.

Garnish:
- Transfer the cauliflower hummus to a serving bowl. Garnish with chopped fresh parsley and drizzle with extra olive oil if desired.

Serve:
- Serve the Keto Cauliflower Hummus with your favorite low-carb dippers, such as cucumber slices, bell pepper strips, or low-carb crackers.

This Keto Cauliflower Hummus is a delicious and satisfying dip that provides the creamy texture and savory flavors of traditional hummus without the added carbs. The cauliflower adds a subtle sweetness, and the combination of tahini and spices gives it a rich and authentic taste. Enjoy this low-carb hummus as a snack or appetizer while staying within your keto lifestyle.

Creamy Garlic Parmesan Shrimp

Ingredients:

- 1 pound large shrimp, peeled and deveined
- 2 tablespoons unsalted butter
- 4 cloves garlic, minced
- 1 cup heavy cream
- 1/2 cup grated Parmesan cheese
- 1 teaspoon Italian seasoning
- Salt and pepper, to taste
- Fresh parsley, chopped (for garnish)
- Lemon wedges (for serving)

Instructions:

Prepare Shrimp:
- Pat the shrimp dry with paper towels and season with salt and pepper.

Sauté Shrimp:
- In a large skillet, melt butter over medium-high heat. Add the shrimp and cook for 1-2 minutes per side until they turn pink. Remove the shrimp from the skillet and set aside.

Make Creamy Sauce:
- In the same skillet, add minced garlic and sauté for about 30 seconds until fragrant. Pour in the heavy cream, Parmesan cheese, and Italian seasoning. Stir continuously until the cheese is melted and the sauce thickens.

Return Shrimp to Skillet:
- Return the cooked shrimp to the skillet and toss them in the creamy sauce, ensuring they are well-coated. Cook for an additional 1-2 minutes until the shrimp are heated through.

Adjust Seasoning:
- Taste the sauce and adjust the seasoning with salt and pepper if needed.

Garnish and Serve:
- Garnish the Creamy Garlic Parmesan Shrimp with chopped fresh parsley. Serve the shrimp over pasta, cauliflower rice, or with a side of vegetables. Optionally, serve with lemon wedges for a burst of citrus flavor.

This Creamy Garlic Parmesan Shrimp dish is a decadent and flavorful option that can be served as a main course or over your favorite low-carb accompaniment. The rich and creamy sauce, combined with the garlicky shrimp and Parmesan, creates a delightful combination of flavors. Enjoy this quick and satisfying meal!

Keto Chocolate Avocado Smoothie

Ingredients:

- 1 ripe avocado, peeled and pitted
- 1 cup unsweetened almond milk or any low-carb milk alternative
- 2 tablespoons unsweetened cocoa powder
- 1-2 tablespoons powdered erythritol or any keto-friendly sweetener, adjust to taste
- 1/2 teaspoon vanilla extract
- 1 cup ice cubes
- Optional: 1-2 tablespoons heavy cream for added creaminess

Instructions:

Blend Ingredients:
- In a blender, combine the ripe avocado, almond milk, cocoa powder, powdered erythritol, vanilla extract, and ice cubes.

Blend Until Smooth:
- Blend the ingredients until smooth and creamy. If the smoothie is too thick, you can add more almond milk or water to reach your desired consistency.

Adjust Sweetness:
- Taste the smoothie and adjust the sweetness by adding more powdered erythritol if necessary.

Optional: Add Heavy Cream:
- If you want an extra creamy texture, add 1-2 tablespoons of heavy cream and blend again.

Serve:
- Pour the Keto Chocolate Avocado Smoothie into a glass and serve immediately.

This smoothie is not only low in carbs but also a great way to incorporate healthy fats from avocados into your diet. The combination of chocolate and avocado creates a decadent and satisfying treat. Feel free to customize the smoothie by adding a scoop of keto-friendly protein powder or a handful of spinach for added nutrients. Enjoy this delicious and keto-friendly chocolate avocado smoothie!

Cabbage and Sausage Skillet

Ingredients:

- 1 pound smoked sausage, sliced into rounds
- 1 small head of cabbage, thinly sliced
- 1 onion, thinly sliced
- 2 cloves garlic, minced
- 2 tablespoons olive oil or butter
- Salt and pepper, to taste
- Optional: Paprika, caraway seeds, or red pepper flakes for added flavor

Instructions:

Cook Sausage:
- In a large skillet, heat olive oil or butter over medium heat. Add the sliced smoked sausage and cook until browned on both sides. Remove the sausage from the skillet and set aside.

Sauté Vegetables:
- In the same skillet, add sliced onion and minced garlic. Sauté until the onion is translucent and aromatic.

Add Cabbage:
- Add the thinly sliced cabbage to the skillet. Toss to combine with the onions and garlic.

Cook Until Tender:
- Continue cooking the cabbage, stirring occasionally, until it wilts and becomes tender. This may take about 8-10 minutes.

Return Sausage:
- Return the cooked sausage to the skillet and toss with the cabbage. Allow everything to cook together for an additional 2-3 minutes to combine the flavors.

Season:
- Season the cabbage and sausage with salt, pepper, and any optional seasonings such as paprika, caraway seeds, or red pepper flakes. Adjust the seasoning to taste.

Serve:
- Serve the Cabbage and Sausage Skillet hot. Optionally, garnish with fresh herbs like parsley.

This Cabbage and Sausage Skillet is a hearty and low-carb dish that comes together quickly. The combination of cabbage and smoked sausage creates a flavorful and satisfying meal. Feel free to customize the recipe by adding your favorite seasonings or additional vegetables. Enjoy!

Keto Broccoli and Cheese Stuffed Chicken Breast

Ingredients:

- 4 boneless, skinless chicken breasts
- Salt and pepper, to taste
- 1 cup steamed broccoli, chopped
- 1 cup shredded cheddar cheese (or your favorite cheese)
- 1/2 cup cream cheese, softened
- 1 teaspoon garlic powder
- 1 teaspoon onion powder
- 1/2 teaspoon paprika
- 1 tablespoon olive oil
- Optional: Chopped fresh parsley for garnish

Instructions:

Preheat Oven:
- Preheat your oven to 375°F (190°C).

Butterfly Chicken Breasts:
- Butterfly each chicken breast by cutting horizontally through the thickest part, creating a pocket without cutting all the way through.

Season Chicken:
- Season the inside of each chicken breast with salt and pepper.

Make Broccoli and Cheese Filling:
- In a bowl, combine the chopped steamed broccoli, shredded cheddar cheese, softened cream cheese, garlic powder, onion powder, and paprika. Mix until well combined.

Stuff Chicken Breasts:
- Spoon the broccoli and cheese mixture into the pocket of each chicken breast, pressing it down gently.

Secure with Toothpicks:
- If needed, secure the opening with toothpicks to keep the filling inside.

Season Outside:
- Season the outside of each stuffed chicken breast with salt and pepper.

Sear Chicken:
- In an oven-safe skillet, heat olive oil over medium-high heat. Sear the stuffed chicken breasts for 2-3 minutes on each side until golden brown.

Bake:

- Transfer the skillet to the preheated oven and bake for 20-25 minutes or until the chicken is cooked through and the cheese is melted and bubbly.

Garnish and Serve:
- Garnish with chopped fresh parsley if desired. Serve the Keto Broccoli and Cheese Stuffed Chicken Breast hot.

This Keto Broccoli and Cheese Stuffed Chicken Breast is a flavorful and cheesy dish that's low in carbs. The combination of tender chicken, creamy filling, and the slight crunch of broccoli creates a satisfying and comforting meal. Enjoy this keto-friendly dinner option!

Avocado Bacon and Egg Salad

Ingredients:

- 4 hard-boiled eggs, peeled and chopped
- 2 ripe avocados, peeled, pitted, and diced
- 6 slices bacon, cooked until crispy and crumbled
- 2 tablespoons mayonnaise
- 1 tablespoon Dijon mustard
- 1 tablespoon lemon juice
- Salt and pepper, to taste
- Chopped fresh chives or green onions (for garnish, optional)

Instructions:

Prepare Eggs:
- Hard-boil the eggs, cool them under cold water, peel, and chop them into bite-sized pieces.

Cook Bacon:
- Cook the bacon until it's crispy. Once cooked, crumble it into small pieces.

Prepare Avocado:
- Peel, pit, and dice the ripe avocados.

Make Dressing:
- In a small bowl, mix together mayonnaise, Dijon mustard, and lemon juice to create the dressing. Adjust the consistency by adding more mayo or lemon juice if needed.

Combine Ingredients:
- In a large bowl, gently combine the chopped hard-boiled eggs, diced avocados, and crumbled bacon.

Add Dressing:
- Pour the dressing over the egg, avocado, and bacon mixture. Gently toss to coat everything evenly.

Season:
- Season the salad with salt and pepper to taste. Be mindful of the salt as the bacon may already add saltiness.

Garnish:
- Garnish with chopped fresh chives or green onions if desired.

Serve:
- Serve the Avocado Bacon and Egg Salad immediately as a side dish, on top of greens, or as a filling for lettuce wraps.

This Avocado Bacon and Egg Salad is a flavorful and satisfying dish that works well as a quick lunch or a side for dinner. The combination of creamy avocado, smoky bacon, and the protein punch from eggs makes it a well-balanced and delicious option. Enjoy!

Zucchini Noodles with Creamy Alfredo Sauce

Ingredients:

- 4 medium-sized zucchinis, spiralized into noodles
- 2 tablespoons unsalted butter
- 2 cloves garlic, minced
- 1 cup heavy cream
- 1 cup grated Parmesan cheese
- Salt and pepper, to taste
- Fresh parsley, chopped (for garnish, optional)

Instructions:

Prepare Zucchini Noodles:
- Spiralize the zucchinis into noodles using a spiralizer. If you don't have a spiralizer, you can use a vegetable peeler to create long, thin strips.

Cook Zucchini Noodles:
- In a large skillet, melt the butter over medium heat. Add the minced garlic and sauté for about 30 seconds until fragrant. Add the zucchini noodles to the skillet and toss for 2-3 minutes until they are just tender. Be careful not to overcook, as zucchini noodles can become too soft.

Make Creamy Alfredo Sauce:
- Pour the heavy cream into the skillet with the zucchini noodles. Stir in the grated Parmesan cheese and continue stirring until the cheese is melted and the sauce is creamy. Season with salt and pepper to taste.

Garnish:
- Garnish the Zucchini Noodles with Creamy Alfredo Sauce with chopped fresh parsley if desired.

Serve:
- Serve the zucchini noodles immediately, either as a side dish or a main course.

This dish provides the creamy goodness of Alfredo sauce without the carbs from traditional pasta. Zucchini noodles, or zoodles, make for a light and refreshing alternative. This recipe is not only low-carb but also gluten-free and keto-friendly. Customize it by adding grilled chicken, shrimp, or your favorite vegetables for a complete and satisfying meal. Enjoy!

Keto Lemon Blueberry Cheesecake Bars

Ingredients:

For the Crust:

- 1 1/2 cups almond flour
- 1/4 cup unsweetened shredded coconut
- 1/4 cup melted butter
- 2 tablespoons powdered erythritol or any keto-friendly sweetener
- 1 teaspoon vanilla extract
- Pinch of salt

For the Cheesecake Filling:

- 16 oz (2 blocks) cream cheese, softened
- 1/2 cup powdered erythritol or any keto-friendly sweetener
- 2 large eggs
- 1 teaspoon vanilla extract
- Zest of 1 lemon
- Juice of 1 lemon

For the Blueberry Swirl:

- 1/2 cup fresh or frozen blueberries
- 1 tablespoon powdered erythritol or any keto-friendly sweetener

Instructions:

Preheat Oven:
- Preheat your oven to 325°F (163°C). Line a square baking dish with parchment paper, leaving an overhang for easy removal.

Make the Crust:
- In a bowl, combine almond flour, shredded coconut, melted butter, powdered erythritol, vanilla extract, and a pinch of salt. Press the mixture evenly into the bottom of the prepared baking dish.

Bake Crust:

- Bake the crust in the preheated oven for 10-12 minutes or until it's lightly golden. Remove from the oven and let it cool slightly.

Prepare Cheesecake Filling:
- In a large bowl, beat the softened cream cheese until smooth. Add powdered erythritol, eggs, vanilla extract, lemon zest, and lemon juice. Beat until well combined and smooth.

Make Blueberry Swirl:
- In a small saucepan, heat the blueberries and powdered erythritol over medium heat until the berries break down and release their juices. Mash them with a fork and simmer for a few minutes until the mixture thickens slightly.

Assemble Cheesecake Bars:
- Pour the cream cheese mixture over the baked crust. Spoon dollops of the blueberry mixture on top. Use a toothpick or a knife to create a swirl pattern.

Bake:
- Bake in the preheated oven for 30-35 minutes or until the edges are set, and the center is slightly jiggly.

Chill:
- Allow the cheesecake bars to cool in the pan, then refrigerate for at least 4 hours or overnight to set.

Slice and Serve:
- Once fully chilled, lift the cheesecake out of the pan using the parchment paper overhang. Slice into bars and serve.

These Keto Lemon Blueberry Cheesecake Bars offer a perfect combination of tangy lemon, sweet blueberries, and creamy cheesecake—all while being low in carbs. Enjoy this guilt-free dessert as a delightful treat on your keto journey!

Cauliflower Tots

Ingredients:

- 3 cups cauliflower florets, finely chopped
- 1 large egg
- 1 cup shredded cheddar cheese
- 1/4 cup grated Parmesan cheese
- 1/4 cup almond flour
- 2 tablespoons fresh parsley, chopped (optional)
- 1 teaspoon garlic powder
- 1/2 teaspoon onion powder
- Salt and pepper, to taste
- Cooking spray or oil for greasing

Instructions:

Preheat Oven:
- Preheat your oven to 400°F (200°C). Grease a baking sheet with cooking spray or oil.

Prepare Cauliflower:
- Steam the cauliflower until it's tender. Once cooked, let it cool slightly, then place it in a clean kitchen towel and squeeze out excess moisture.

Combine Ingredients:
- In a large bowl, combine the chopped cauliflower, egg, cheddar cheese, Parmesan cheese, almond flour, fresh parsley (if using), garlic powder, onion powder, salt, and pepper. Mix well until the ingredients are evenly combined.

Form Tots:
- Take about a tablespoon of the mixture and shape it into a tot or small cylinder. Place it on the prepared baking sheet. Repeat with the remaining mixture, leaving some space between each tot.

Bake:
- Bake in the preheated oven for 20-25 minutes or until the tots are golden brown and crispy.

Broil (Optional):
- If you want extra crispiness, you can broil the tots for an additional 1-2 minutes, but keep a close eye to prevent burning.

Serve:

- Allow the Cauliflower Tots to cool slightly before serving. Enjoy them with your favorite dipping sauce.

These Cauliflower Tots are a tasty and healthier alternative to traditional tater tots, and they're perfect for those following a keto or low-carb lifestyle. Feel free to customize the recipe by adding spices or herbs of your choice. Enjoy this guilt-free snack!

Keto Garlic Butter Shrimp

Ingredients:

- 1 pound large shrimp, peeled and deveined
- 2 tablespoons unsalted butter
- 3 cloves garlic, minced
- 1 tablespoon fresh parsley, chopped
- 1 tablespoon lemon juice
- Salt and pepper, to taste
- Red pepper flakes (optional, for a bit of heat)

Instructions:

Prepare Shrimp:
- Pat the shrimp dry with paper towels and season with salt and pepper.

Cook Shrimp:
- In a large skillet, melt the butter over medium heat. Add the minced garlic and sauté for about 30 seconds until fragrant.

Add Shrimp:
- Add the seasoned shrimp to the skillet and cook for 2-3 minutes on each side or until they turn pink and opaque.

Season:
- Season the shrimp with additional salt and pepper to taste. If you like a bit of heat, you can add red pepper flakes at this point.

Finish with Lemon Juice:
- Squeeze lemon juice over the shrimp and toss to coat evenly.

Garnish:
- Garnish the Keto Garlic Butter Shrimp with chopped fresh parsley.

Serve:
- Serve the shrimp immediately as a standalone dish or over cauliflower rice for a complete keto meal.

This Keto Garlic Butter Shrimp is a simple yet flavorful dish that comes together in minutes. The combination of garlic, butter, and lemon enhances the natural sweetness of the shrimp, creating a delicious and satisfying meal. Feel free to customize the recipe by adding your favorite herbs or serving it with low-carb veggies. Enjoy!

Keto Chicken Fajita Bowls

Ingredients:

For the Chicken Marinade:

- 1.5 pounds boneless, skinless chicken breasts, sliced into strips
- 3 tablespoons olive oil
- 2 tablespoons lime juice
- 1 teaspoon ground cumin
- 1 teaspoon chili powder
- 1 teaspoon paprika
- 1 teaspoon garlic powder
- 1/2 teaspoon onion powder
- Salt and pepper, to taste

For the Fajita Bowls:

- 1 bell pepper, thinly sliced
- 1 onion, thinly sliced
- 2 tablespoons olive oil
- Salt and pepper, to taste
- Cauliflower rice or lettuce leaves (for serving)
- Guacamole, salsa, sour cream, shredded cheese (for topping)

Instructions:

Marinate the Chicken:

In a bowl, whisk together the olive oil, lime juice, ground cumin, chili powder, paprika, garlic powder, onion powder, salt, and pepper to create the marinade. Add the sliced chicken to the marinade, ensuring each piece is well coated. Let it marinate for at least 30 minutes in the refrigerator.

Cook the Chicken:

Heat a skillet over medium-high heat. Add a bit of olive oil.

Cook the marinated chicken strips in the skillet for 5-7 minutes or until they are cooked through and slightly browned. Remove from the skillet and set aside.

Cook the Vegetables:

In the same skillet, add a bit more olive oil if needed. Add the sliced bell pepper and onion.
Sauté the vegetables until they are tender and slightly caramelized. Season with salt and pepper to taste.

Assemble the Bowls:

Serve the cooked chicken and vegetables over cauliflower rice or lettuce leaves for a low-carb option.
Top the bowls with guacamole, salsa, sour cream, shredded cheese, or any other keto-friendly toppings of your choice.

These Keto Chicken Fajita Bowls are customizable and perfect for a low-carb lifestyle.

You can adjust the toppings based on your preferences, and the combination of

seasoned chicken and sautéed vegetables creates a satisfying and flavorful meal.

Enjoy!

Cheesy Cauliflower Breadsticks

Ingredients:

For the Cauliflower Crust:

- 1 medium-sized cauliflower, riced (about 3 cups)
- 1 cup mozzarella cheese, shredded
- 1 large egg
- 1 teaspoon dried oregano
- 1 teaspoon garlic powder
- Salt and pepper, to taste

For the Topping:

- 1 cup mozzarella cheese, shredded
- 1/4 cup Parmesan cheese, grated
- 1 teaspoon dried oregano
- 1/2 teaspoon garlic powder
- Marinara sauce (for dipping)

Instructions:

Prepare the Cauliflower Crust:

Preheat your oven to 425°F (220°C). Line a baking sheet with parchment paper.
Rice the Cauliflower:
- Cut the cauliflower into florets and pulse in a food processor until it resembles rice.

Cook Cauliflower:
- Place the riced cauliflower in a microwave-safe bowl and microwave for 4-5 minutes. Allow it to cool for a few minutes.

Form the Cauliflower Dough:
- In a bowl, combine the microwaved cauliflower, 1 cup shredded mozzarella, egg, oregano, garlic powder, salt, and pepper. Mix until well combined.

Shape the Crust:

- Transfer the cauliflower mixture to the prepared baking sheet and spread it into a rectangle or circle, forming the crust.

Bake:
- Bake the cauliflower crust in the preheated oven for 15-20 minutes or until it's golden brown and set.

Add Toppings:

Remove the crust from the oven and sprinkle it with 1 cup shredded mozzarella, grated Parmesan, dried oregano, and garlic powder.

Return to Oven:
- Place the crust back in the oven and bake for an additional 5-7 minutes or until the cheese is melted and bubbly.

Broil (Optional):
- If you want a golden and crispy top, broil for 1-2 minutes, keeping a close eye to prevent burning.

Slice and Serve:
- Allow the Cheesy Cauliflower Breadsticks to cool for a few minutes before slicing. Serve with marinara sauce for dipping.

These Cheesy Cauliflower Breadsticks are a delicious and satisfying keto-friendly snack or appetizer. The cauliflower crust is flavorful and holds up well, and the melted cheese on top adds a gooey and indulgent touch. Enjoy this low-carb alternative to traditional breadsticks!

Keto Chocolate Peanut Butter Fat Bombs

Ingredients:

- 1/2 cup coconut oil, melted
- 1/2 cup unsweetened peanut butter
- 1/4 cup unsweetened cocoa powder
- 2 tablespoons powdered erythritol or any keto-friendly sweetener
- 1/2 teaspoon vanilla extract
- Pinch of salt

Instructions:

- Prepare Mixture:
  - In a bowl, combine melted coconut oil, unsweetened peanut butter, cocoa powder, powdered erythritol, vanilla extract, and a pinch of salt. Mix until well combined.
- Fill Molds:
  - Pour the mixture into silicone molds or mini cupcake liners, dividing it evenly.
- Chill:
  - Place the molds in the freezer and let the fat bombs set for at least 1-2 hours or until they are firm.
- Remove and Serve:
  - Once the fat bombs are set, pop them out of the molds. If you used cupcake liners, you can simply peel them away.
- Store:
  - Store the Keto Chocolate Peanut Butter Fat Bombs in an airtight container in the freezer. They can be kept for several weeks.

These fat bombs are a great way to satisfy your sweet cravings while providing a dose of healthy fats. The combination of chocolate and peanut butter is a classic and indulgent flavor pairing. Enjoy these treats in moderation as part of your low-carb or keto lifestyle!

Grilled Portobello Mushrooms with Balsamic Glaze

Ingredients:

For the Marinade:

- 4 large portobello mushrooms, stems removed
- 1/4 cup balsamic vinegar
- 3 tablespoons olive oil
- 2 cloves garlic, minced
- 1 teaspoon dried thyme or rosemary
- Salt and pepper, to taste

For the Balsamic Glaze:

- 1/2 cup balsamic vinegar
- 1 tablespoon low-carb sweetener (such as erythritol or stevia), optional

Optional Toppings:

- Fresh parsley, chopped
- Feta or goat cheese, crumbled
- Cherry tomatoes, sliced

Instructions:

Marinate and Grill Portobello Mushrooms:

In a bowl, whisk together balsamic vinegar, olive oil, minced garlic, dried thyme or rosemary, salt, and pepper to create the marinade.
Place the portobello mushrooms in a shallow dish and pour the marinade over them. Allow them to marinate for at least 30 minutes, turning them occasionally to coat evenly.
Preheat your grill or grill pan over medium-high heat. Grill the portobello mushrooms for about 4-5 minutes per side or until they are tender and have grill marks.

Make Balsamic Glaze:

In a small saucepan, combine 1/2 cup balsamic vinegar and optional low-carb sweetener.

Bring to a simmer over medium heat and let it cook for about 10-15 minutes or until the vinegar has reduced by half and has a syrupy consistency. Stir occasionally.

Assemble and Serve:

Place the grilled portobello mushrooms on a serving plate.

Drizzle the balsamic glaze over the mushrooms.

Garnish with optional toppings such as chopped fresh parsley, crumbled feta or goat cheese, and sliced cherry tomatoes.

Serve the Grilled Portobello Mushrooms with Balsamic Glaze immediately.

This dish is not only delicious but also versatile. You can enjoy the grilled portobello mushrooms on their own, as a side dish, or even as a burger substitute. The balsamic glaze adds a sweet and tangy flavor that complements the earthy taste of the mushrooms. Enjoy!

www.ingramcontent.com/pod-product-compliance
Lightning Source LLC
LaVergne TN
LVHW081610060526
838201LV00054B/2170